Saskatchewan

Jennifer D. B. Lackey

Scholastic Canada Ltd.

Toronto New York London Auckland Sydney
Mexico City New Delhi Hong Kong Buenos Aires

Visual Credits

Cover: Ron Erwin ©AllCanadaPhotos.com; p I.: Natural Moments Photography/Darwin Wigge/First Light; p. III: Grambo/First Light; p. IV: Terry Davis/Shutterstock Inc. (top), D. Robert & Lorri Franz/Corbis (middle), Richard Hamilton Smith/Corbis (right); pp. 2-3: Robert Postma/First Light; p. 3: Mark Duffy/Alamy; p. 4: Ron Erwin ©AllCanadaPhotos.com; p. 5: John Sylvester Photography; p. 6: Chad Coombs/First Light; p. 7: Bill Brooks/Alamy (bottom), Mark Duffy/Alamy (top); p. 8: CP Photo/Prince Albert Daily Herald - Craig Ellingson; p. 9: Wayne Lynch/All Canada Photos; p. 10: Robin Karpan/Parkland Publishing; p. 11: Dorling Kindersley; p. 12: Paul Kane, *Assiniboine Hunting Buffalo* c. 1851-1856, National Gallery of Canada, Ottawa. p. 13: Horace T. Martin, F.Z.S.Glenbow Museum; pp. 14-15: O.B. Buell/Library and Archives Canada/PA-118768; p. 16: Eric Isselée/Shutterstock Inc.; p. 17: Illustrated War News, May 30, 1885; p. 18: Duffin and Co./Bibliothèque et Archives Canada/C-052177 (right), Library and Archives Canada/PA-178147 (left); p. 19: Canadian Pacific Railway Company; Gleason, H.W. (top); p. 20: Gleason, H.W. (top), A.G.E. Foto Stock/First Light (bottom); p. 21: Doukhobors/Library and Archives Canada/C-008888 (top), Library and Archives Canada (bottom); p. 24: Grambo/First Light; p. 25: Picture Arts/First Light (top), Dave Reede/First Light (bottom); p. 26: Natural Moments Photography/Darwin Wigge/First Light; p. 27: Mike Grandmaison/First Light; p. 28: James Brady (bottom), KdEdesign/Shutterstock Inc. (top); p. 29: Karen Kasmauski/Corbis (bottom), W.E. GARRETT/National Geographic Stock (top); p. 30: Ken Faught/CP Images; p. 31: CFL PHOTO/L. MacDougal; p. 32: Bettmann/Corbis (bottom); p. 33: Scott Prokop/iStock (left), Feiler Fotodesign/Stock Food Canada (right); p. 34: Watts/Hall Inc/First Light (top), 22DigiTal/Alamy (top), CTV/Prairie Pants Productions (bottom); p. 36: O.B. Buell/Library and Archives Canada/C-001873 (right), O.B. Buell/Library and Archives Canada/C-001875 (left); p. 37: Graham Tim/Corbis Sygma; p. 38: W. E. Hook; p. 39: Canadian Illustrated News, Vol. XI, No. 6, Page 88, Reproduced from Library and Archives Canada's website Images in the News: Canadian Illustrated News, (bottom), Notman, William and Son, Montreal, Quebec, (top); pp. 40-41 and back cover: J. Baylor Roberts/National Geographic Stock; p. 41: Thomas Kitchin & Victoria Hurst/First Light (top); p. 42: Cameron, Duncan/Library and Archives Canada/C-036222; p. 43: Steve Byland/Shutterstock Inc. (top), Chas/Shutterstock Inc. (bottom).

Produced by Plan B Book Packagers
Editorial: Ellen Rodger
Design: Rosie Gowsell-Pattison
Special thanks to consultant and editor Terrance Cox, adjunct professor, Brock University;
Jim Chernishenko; Nancy Hodgson and Tanya Rutledge.

Library and Archives Canada Cataloguing in Publication

Lackey, Jennifer, 1969-
Saskatchewan / Jennifer D.B. Lackey.

(Canada close up)
ISBN 978-0-545-98902-2

1. Saskatchewan—Juvenile literature. I. Title.
II. Series: Canada close up (Toronto, Ont.)

FC3511.2.L33 2009   j971.2   C2008-906865-3

ISBN-10 0-545-98902-7

6 5 4 3 2 1   Printed in Canada   09 10 11 12 13 14

Contents

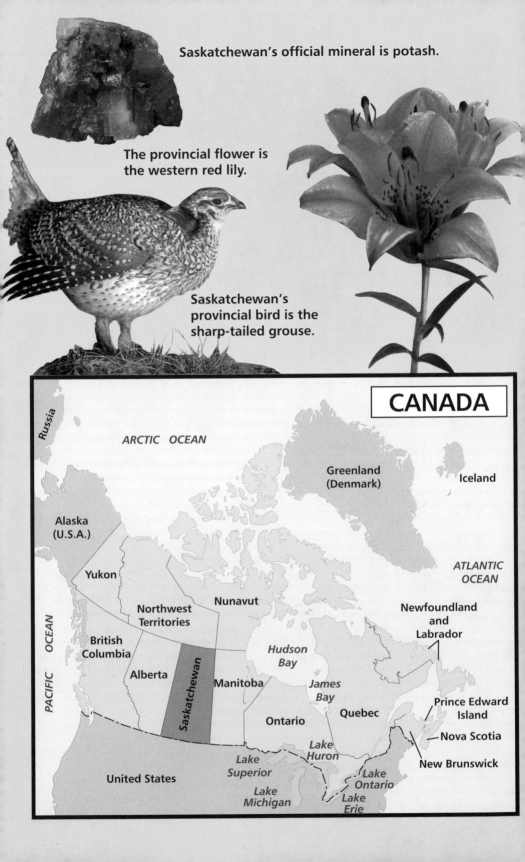

Saskatchewan's official mineral is potash.

The provincial flower is the western red lily.

Saskatchewan's provincial bird is the sharp-tailed grouse.

CANADA

Russia

ARCTIC OCEAN

Greenland (Denmark)

Iceland

Alaska (U.S.A.)

Yukon

Northwest Territories

Nunavut

ATLANTIC OCEAN

Newfoundland and Labrador

PACIFIC OCEAN

British Columbia

Alberta

Saskatchewan

Hudson Bay

Manitoba

James Bay

Prince Edward Island

Nova Scotia

Ontario

Quebec

New Brunswick

United States

Lake Superior

Lake Huron

Lake Michigan

Lake Ontario

Lake Erie

Welcome to Saskatchewan!

When people think of Saskatchewan, they often think of massive fields of grain and long roads stretching as far as the eye can see. After all, Saskatchewan is one of Canada's **prairie** provinces. But there is more to the province than just wheat fields.

Saskatchewan also boasts badlands, hills, enormous forests and thousands of lakes and rivers. It has exciting cities and quiet towns. It has mines and factories as well as farms.

Saskatchewan has made many important contributions to our country's history, government and culture since it became a province in 1905. When you get to know more about Saskatchewan, you will find many things to surprise you.

Chapter 1
Wide Open Skies

Scientists who study the Earth identify places that have different land, weather, plants and animals. They called these areas **ecozones**. Saskatchewan has four ecozones. They are the prairie, the boreal plain, the boreal shield and the taiga shield.

The prairie

The prairie grasslands stretch across the southern part of the province. Hundreds of years ago, this flat area was covered in wild grasses. It is now mostly farmland where grain such as wheat and rye is grown. Other crops such as barley, oats and canola, and pulses such as lentils, are also grown on prairie farms.

The aurora borealis (northern lights) is a spectacular sight in the Saskatchewan night sky. There is very little reflection from city lights to reduce its brightness.

Few trees grow on the prairie because it does not get enough rain. The western prairie is drier than the eastern part. Both are very cold in the winter. Temperatures sometimes drop as low as -50 degrees Celsius. It can be very hot in the summer as well, occasionally rising to a sweltering 40 degrees Celsius.

Some natural prairie grasslands, like these, now **protected** in Grasslands National Park, look much as they did before settlers came.

A home for gophers

Mice, rabbits, coyotes, foxes and badgers live on the prairie. Many shelter in underground homes because there are very few trees. Richardson's ground squirrels, also known as gophers, dig large burrows with many complicated passageways and tunnels.

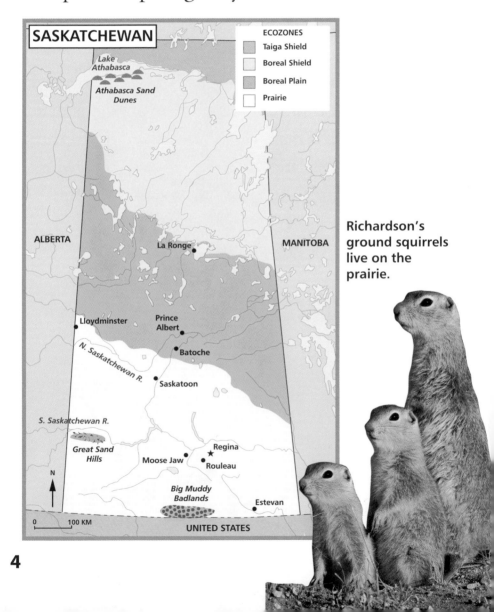

SASKATCHEWAN

ECOZONES
- Taiga Shield
- Boreal Shield
- Boreal Plain
- Prairie

Lake Athabasca

Athabasca Sand Dunes

ALBERTA

La Ronge

MANITOBA

Lloydminster

Prince Albert

N. Saskatchewan R.

Batoche

Saskatoon

S. Saskatchewan R.

Great Sand Hills

Moose Jaw

Regina

Rouleau

Big Muddy Badlands

Estevan

N

0   100 KM

UNITED STATES

Richardson's ground squirrels live on the prairie.

A rock outcrop rises from the Big Muddy Badlands in southwestern Saskatchewan. The area is rich in fossils and dinosaur bones.

Dinosaur territory

Many people think Saskatchewan is flat, but the province is really a mix of plains, hills, valleys and glacial rock. The Big Muddy Badlands in southern Saskatchewan were created when melting glaciers formed fast-flowing rivers that carved through rock. Early explorers called the area "badlands" because the silty soil turned into slippery mud when wet. This made them bad lands to travel through. The area is not "bad" for geologists and **paleontologists**. Many dinosaur bones have been unearthed here.

The boreal plain

North of the prairie lies the boreal plain. This plain reaches across the centre of the province. Temperatures here are cooler in the summer months than on the prairie and the winters are longer. More rain and snow falls, and both grasses and trees thrive. In the southern part of the boreal plain, trees such as aspen, poplar and birch grow. In the northern part, the forests are mostly spruce and pine.

This area is rich in wildlife such as deer, owls, wolves, moose, caribou, beavers, loons, grouse, geese and ducks. There are many lakes full of fish. Many areas of forest have been cut down by loggers. The trees are used for lumber and to make paper.

Wolves are native to Saskatchewan's boreal forests.

Trees are cut for wood and paper products.

The Saskatchewan River flows eastward across Saskatchewan and into the neighbouring province of Manitoba. It is a major river with two branches, the North Saskatchewan and the South Saskatchewan.

The boreal shield

The boreal shield has thicker forests than the boreal plain. The trees here are mostly evergreen spruce and pine. The northern part of this ecozone lies over a rock formation called the Canadian Shield. The Canadian Shield is very old rock that is covered by a thin layer of soil. The land of the boreal shield has gentle hills and gets more rain than the boreal plain or the prairie. Temperatures are cooler in the summer months than they are farther south, and the winters can be quite cold for longer periods of time.

Large mammals such as wolves and black bears live in boreal shield forests. Portions of these forests are protected from logging by the government. In dry years, fires sometimes burn parts of the forest. This is a natural part of its life cycle.

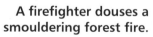
A firefighter douses a smouldering forest fire.

The taiga shield

The taiga shield is in the northeastern corner of the province. Here the boreal forest becomes thinner in the dry cold nearer to the Arctic. The trees are spruce and pine, but they are spaced further apart. There is less wildlife here than in any other area in Saskatchewan. It is home to animals such as arctic foxes and caribou, and birds like rock ptarmigan and arctic terns.

Hoarfrost, or frozen water vapour, clings to trees in a northern Saskatchewan forest.

Shifting sands

Most people don't imagine sand dunes when they think of Saskatchewan. But they're here, and they're massive.

The Athabasca Sand Dunes are located in the northwest corner of the province, along the edge of Lake Athabasca. Some of them are 30 metres high! They were created during the last ice age, about 8000 years ago, and are the northernmost sand dunes in the world. The area is protected as a provincial park. A second set of dunes, called the Great Sand Hills, is south of the South Saskatchewan River and just east of Alberta. These dunes were created about 10,000 years ago by retreating ice-age glaciers.

The Athabasca Sand Dunes were formed when retreating glaciers ground sandstone into powder. Ten plant species found nowhere else in the world grow here.

The scoop on Saskatchewan

- The province's name comes from the Cree word for swift-flowing, *kisiskâciwani*. It refers to the Saskatchewan River, a major Canadian waterway. The North Saskatchewan River has been named a Canadian Heritage River because it was so important to the fur trade. It flows from mountain glaciers in Alberta and joins the South Saskatchewan River to form the largest river system in western Canada.

- Saskatchewan is rich in potash, uranium, coal, oil and natural gas.

- Even though it's called a prairie province, half of Saskatchewan is actually covered in forest.

- Saskatchewan has more than 100,000 lakes. The largest, Lake Athabasca, straddles Alberta and Saskatchewan. The world's biggest lake trout – a whopping 46 kilograms – was caught here.

Artist Paul Kane painted *Assiniboine Chasing Buffalo* in 1850.

Chapter 2
Prairie to Province

Before Europeans arrived, many Aboriginal groups lived in what is now Saskatchewan – some for thousands of years. Each had different languages and laws. Some were **allies**, while others were enemies. Today the Aboriginal peoples in south and central Saskatchewan are known as the Plains peoples. They include the Assiniboine, Plains Cree, Plains Ojibwa, Blackfoot and Gros Ventre. These people were **bison** hunters who followed migrating herds across the plains. The Aboriginal peoples of northern Saskatchewan, such as the Chipewyans and the Woodland Cree, fished and hunted elk, moose and deer.

The fur trade

The fur trade was a major industry in North America for hundreds of years. Animal furs were used in Europe to make hats and coats. These furs were valuable. The desire for riches brought many explorers west in the 1600s and 1700s. They worked for fur trading companies and used Aboriginal guides to help them find their way. These explorers mapped the territory and gave us many of our present-day names for rivers, lakes and other natural features.

In Europe, sturdy hats made from beaver felt were fashionable. Men wore different styles that suited their professions or status in society.

Kelsey's trail

In 1670 King Charles II of England gave the Hudson's Bay Company (HBC) control of **Rupert's Land,** a territory that included most of what is now Saskatchewan. This gave the English trading company a monopoly, or sole control, over the fur trade in the west.

In 1690 the HBC sent young Henry Kelsey to explore the territory and find Aboriginal trading partners. Kelsey spent two years travelling through what is now Manitoba and Saskatchewan, becoming the first European to reach Saskatchewan.

In 1774 Hudson's Bay Company explorer Samuel Hearne set up the company's first Saskatchewan outpost at Cumberland House, on the Saskatchewan River. Other posts followed. A rival trading company, the North West Company, began competing with the Hudson's Bay Company in 1780. As the fur trade moved west, French, Scottish and English traders came with it. Many traders had families with Aboriginal women, and their children became known as the **Métis**.

Cree chief Mistahimaskwa, or Big Bear (5th from left), and others, trade at Fort Pitt, Saskatchewan.

Big Bear refused to sign a **treaty** in 1876 surrendering Cree lands, but changed his mind when his people began to starve.

The disappearing buffalo

For centuries bison were the main food source for Aboriginal peoples of the plains. In well-organized hunts, herds were corralled or led off cliffs to their deaths. The meat was dried to provide food throughout the year. The hides were used for clothing and shelter, and bones and **sinew** became tools and thread for sewing.

By the 1830s, though, the hunt wasn't just for food or shelter. The Hudson's Bay Company began trading for buffalo hides and robes. And European bison hunters began arriving for sport hunts. The bison herds were so large that no one imagined hunting them would do any harm, but, by the 1880s, the bison were almost **extinct**. Since the Aboriginal peoples of the prairies and the Métis relied on the bison, their way of life changed forever.

Batoche was the scene of the last major battle for Métis independence. The Métis and their Aboriginal allies resisted Canada taking control of the land they had claimed as their own.

The Resistance

Nova Scotia, New Brunswick, Ontario and Quebec joined together as one country – the Dominion of Canada – in 1867. But Rupert's Land was still the property of the Hudson's Bay Company. In 1869 Canada gained control of the area and called it the Northwest Territories. Canadian leaders planned to extend the country from the Atlantic to the Pacific.

This transfer of land from the Hudson's Bay Company angered the Métis who lived in Rupert's Land. No one had consulted them. They wanted to negotiate their own territory and they feared Canada would bring more settlers to take their land.

The Métis fought for their land. In 1869 and 1870 they led armed protests in Manitoba. The Red River Resistance was not fully successful, and many Métis moved west to what is now Saskatchewan. The Métis led another uprising in 1885, called the Northwest Resistance, around Batoche, in central Saskatchewan. Outnumbered, they surrendered to Canadian forces after two months.

Métis political leader Louis Riel was convicted of **treason** in Regina and executed.

Gabriel Dumont was the military leader of the Métis force during the Northwest Resistance. He was able to avoid capture by escaping to the United States.

Treaties, trains and settlers

With the loss of their main food source, the bison, the once-strong Aboriginal peoples were almost starving. The Canadian government wanted to bring settlers to the west and needed their lands. Treaties were drawn up for this purpose. Some Aboriginal groups held out for as long as they could, but by 1880 most were living on parcels of land set aside for them, called reserves.

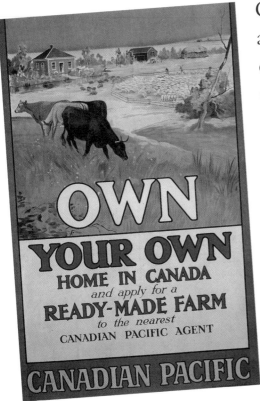

OWN
YOUR OWN
HOME IN CANADA
and apply for a
READY-MADE FARM
to the nearest
CANADIAN PACIFIC AGENT

CANADIAN PACIFIC

Settlers from eastern Canada started arriving. Most came as passengers on the newly built Canadian Pacific Railway. They plowed the prairies and set up homesteads and farms.

Posters advertised the availability of land for farming in Saskatchewan.

After 1885 the railway helped bring settlers west to Saskatchewan. It was also used to transport western grain to the east.

The government also encouraged emigration from Europe with offers of free land. From the 1890s to the late 1920s, thousands of **homesteaders** came from Russia, Ukraine, Scandinavia, Poland and Britain.

Ukrainian settlers built churches with distinctive onion-shaped domes on the prairies.

The breadbasket of Canada

The new homesteaders busted sod, or broke the soil, and made the prairie into vast grain fields. After becoming an official province in 1905, Saskatchewan was soon renowned as "Canada's breadbasket." Prairie towns grew around railway stations where trainloads of wheat were shipped to eastern Canada. There was so much farm work that labourers came by train from the east each summer for harvest season.

Settlers transformed the prairie landscape, building communities and replacing grasslands with fields of wheat.

The dirty thirties

But the good times didn't last. Grain prices fell in the 1920s. Several years of **drought** in the 1930s made the prairies into a dust bowl. Winds blew the precious topsoil away in furious dust blizzards. To make things worse, the **Great Depression** put people out of work in much of the western world. The market for Saskatchewan grain, what little could now be grown, shrank further. The drought lasted nine years. The Depression ended in 1939, with the beginning of World War II.

In the 1930s Saskatchewan was hit harder by drought and the Great Depression than any other province of Canada. These years were called the "dirty thirties" because of the dust storms created by the drought.

So many people were out of work during the Depression that the government created work camps. Conditions in the camps led to the Regina Riot in 1935, when men heading to Ottawa to protest were stopped by police. Two people were killed.

Medicare: a Canadian first

The Depression had a lasting effect on Saskatchewan. Many people could not afford to pay a doctor if they were sick. In 1962 Saskatchewan set up a program that changed health care in Canada. The program made medical care publicly funded, which means it was paid for out of provincial tax dollars. Saskatchewan doctors protested and went on strike, but within ten years the entire country had adopted similar health care plans.

Wild rice grows in a northern Saskatchewan lake.

Chapter 3
Nature's Riches

Farming is still big business in Saskatchewan. Cereal crops are tops, but did you know that the province produces most of Canada's wild rice? This is actually a type of aquatic grass that thrives in northern lakes and is a gourmet delicacy. A large percentage of the wild rice is planted, harvested and sold by Aboriginal peoples in Saskatchewan.

Golden fields

Wheat made Saskatchewan famous. But despite plenty of sunshine and rich soil, it is not easy to grow grain in the province. In good years, there is enough rain. In years of drought, the crops fail because of lack of water.

Canola, an oilseed developed in Canada, is the second-largest crop in the province. Its name comes from "Canadian oil, low acid." It is used to make salad oils and margarine.

In the summer the fields are bright with yellow flowers. Some are canola and some are mustard. Saskatchewan is the world's largest exporter of seeds for making mustard.

A farmer examines his wheat crop. Marquis wheat is a Canadian wheat that was developed 100 years ago especially for the prairies.

Wells pump oil from beneath farm fields near Estevan, Saskatchewan.

Oil and gas

Other things besides food come from the ground in Saskatchewan. The province is rich in minerals and **fossil fuels** too.

Saskatchewan mines produce more uranium than anywhere else in the world. This is a metal used for making electricity in nuclear reactors. Potash is another abundant mineral, used for making soap, glass and fertilizers for crops. Coal and oil are also found here. In fact, Saskatchewan is the second-largest producer of oil in Canada.

(left) Fields of yellow flowering canola extend to the horizon.

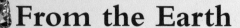

From the Earth

- Saskatchewan grows 54 per cent of Canada's wheat.

- The Esterhazy potash mine in southeastern Saskatchewan is the world's largest.

- Gold is mined near La Ronge in north-central Saskatchewan.

- Diamonds have been found near Prince Albert in central Saskatchewan.

In the mid 1900s, prospectors hunt for gold in La Ronge.

A mining machine chews through potash.

The Key Lake Mine is the largest uranium-producing mine in the world.

In 1998 Sandra Schmirler and her Regina-based team won the first-ever Olympic gold medal in women's curling.

Chapter 4

Prairie Culture

Having fun in Saskatchewan is all about community – sharing good times with friends and family. Throughout the long winter, curling rinks become the social centres of more than 200 communities across the province. Curling is so cool in Saskatchewan that it's the official provincial sport. In 1998 Sandra Schmirler led her team from Regina to win the first-ever Olympic gold medal for women's curling.

Good sports

Saskatchewan has some of the most dedicated sports fans in the country. But the province has only one professional sports team. The Saskatchewan Roughriders, a Canadian Football League team, is based in Regina. Rider fans, known as "Rider Nation," travel from all over the province to cheer their team on. The Roughriders have won the **Grey Cup** three times, but even when they're not having a championship year, Rider fans celebrate Grey Cup games with huge parties.

Roughrider fans are dedicated and not afraid to show their team colours in imaginative ways.

The Regina Pats (pictured above in 1924), are the oldest continuously operating junior hockey league team in the country. Many professional hockey players come from Saskatchewan.

National Hockey League great Gordie Howe was born in Floral, Saskatchewan. "Mr. Hockey" was an outstanding player through 32 seasons of professional hockey.

Pies and perogies

European settlers to Saskatchewan brought their own familiar recipes to the province. German sausage and cabbage rolls and Ukrainian perogies (potato and cheese dumplings) are now popular across the country. Other foods are distinctly Saskatchewanian. Saskatoon berries are small red berries from a large shrub that is native to Saskatchewan. The berries make delicious pies, jams and jellies. Aboriginal peoples used the berries in pemmican, a food made for travelling on the prairies. Pemmican is still made today, but often without the elk, buffalo or deer fat of the original recipes.

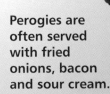

Perogies are often served with fried onions, bacon and sour cream.

Pile o' what?

Saskatchewan isn't just farmland and villages. Regina is the capital and the second–largest city in the province. Its original name was Pile o' Bones because it was where the Cree piled buffalo bones after a hunt. In 1882 it was named Regina (Latin for queen) after Queen Victoria.

Saskatoon is Saskatchewan's biggest city, with a population of almost 214,000. Its name comes from the Cree word for the berry found in the area.

Saskatoon is called the City of Bridges because of the seven bridges that cross the South Saskatchewan River.

Today Regina is much more than a pile of bones. Where once were no trees and little water, it now has many parks, over 350,000 trees and the man-made Wascana Lake.

The television comedy series *Corner Gas* was filmed on sets built in Regina and Rouleau, Saskatchewan. It focused on a group of characters in a small prairie town.

First Nations U!

Saskatchewan has produced some of the most famous First Nations and Métis leaders in Canadian history. Aboriginal peoples here suffered badly with the end of the buffalo hunt and the beginning of European settlement. Today fifteen per cent of Saskatchewan's total population of over one million is of First Nations or Métis heritage. Many are rebuilding their lives and their culture.

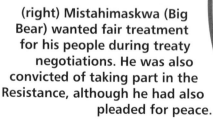

(left) Pitikwahanapiwiyin, or Poundmaker, was a Cree chief who believed the Canadian government did not live up to its treaties. Known as a peacemaker, he tried to prevent his people from joining the Northwest Resistance. Unsuccessful in this, he was held responsible and sent to jail.

(right) Mistahimaskwa (Big Bear) wanted fair treatment for his people during treaty negotiations. He was also convicted of taking part in the Resistance, although he had also pleaded for peace.

The First Nations University of Canada is the country's only Aboriginal-centred university. It has a campus in Regina and offers courses in other Saskatchewan cities and online. Every year it hosts Saskatchewan's biggest powwow. Powwows are colourful get-togethers where dancers, drummers and singers in beaded and feathered costumes compete for prizes. Food booths feature treats such as fry bread, a deep-fried bread dough coated in sugar or piled with meat and spices.

Powwows are modern celebrations that foster pride in Aboriginal heritage.

Chapter 5

Mountie Territory

Saskatchewan has a long history with the law. The **forebears** of today's Mounties, the North West Mounted Police (NWMP), were formed in 1874 as a result of a murderous **rampage** in Saskatchewan by American whisky traders. The Cypress Hills Massacre took place in 1873 on the Saskatchewan–Alberta border. The drunken traders killed more than twenty Assiniboine in their camp. When news of the massacre reached the east, the government of Canada decided to form a national police force to bring order to the west and force the Americans out.

The Mounties began a long trek across the prairies in 1874. Their journey, called the March West, began in Dufferin, Manitoba, and ended in Alberta. They never did bring the Cypress Hills murderers to justice, but they did bring peace to the west.

Sam Steele was one of the best-known members of the North West Mounted Police. He led new recruits on the March West.

The North West Mounted Police trekked west through what is now Saskatchewan in 1874.

Trained in Saskatchewan

The NWMP became the Royal Canadian Mounted Police (RCMP) in 1920. Today, the Mounties are a national police force in every province and territory. They also serve as provincial and municipal police in many provinces, including Saskatchewan. They enforce laws and guard important members of the government, such as the Prime Minister. The training academy is located in Regina. All RCMP cadets come here for 24 weeks of basic training. The academy also has a museum of RCMP history.

Fort Walsh, in Maple Creek, Saskatchewan, became the North West Mounted Police headquarters in 1878. It was later a ranch where, until 1968, the horses for the RCMP's musical ride were raised.

Chapter 6
Points of Pride

▶ The bronze-coloured waters of Little Manitou Lake, southeast of Saskatoon, are so full of **mineral salts** that people float instead of sink.

▶ The largest hailstone in Canada fell near Cedoux in southern Saskatchewan in August 1973. It was 290 grams and about the size of a grapefruit.

▶ In 2004 Tommy Douglas was voted the Greatest Canadian in a national contest. He is called the "father of medicare" because, as the premier of Saskatchewan, he announced a plan in 1962 that made health care available to everyone in the province.

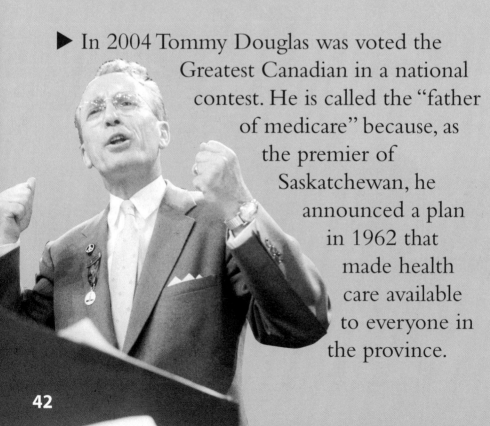

▶ Saskatchewan contains an important migration and breeding area for birds. It is part of the North American Central Flyway – a migration route that follows the Great Plains through the United States and into Canada. Each spring, birds fly north from as far away as Argentina. In the fall, they fly back. Saskatchewan is a major stopping point for about one quarter of all the ducks and geese that use this route. The province's wilderness areas are so vital to the health of North America's wild bird populations that the first bird sanctuary in North America was established here at Last Mountain Lake in 1887.

▶ Saskatchewan is the only province in Canada that does not observe daylight saving time. People here don't turn their clocks forward in the spring or back in the fall.

Hummingbirds (top left) and Canada geese (above) are among the many bird species who use the Central Flyway.

Glossary

allies: Nations or groups of people who support each other in times of peace and war

bison: Large grass-eating prairie mammals often called buffalo

drought: A long period without rainfall

ecozones: Distinct geographic areas with specific climates and plant and animal species

extinct: Describes an animal or plant species that has died out or no longer exists

forebears: Ancestors; the people or group who went before

fossil fuels: Fuels made from coal, oil or natural gas

Great Depression: An international economic crisis (1929-1939) that left many people out of work and very poor

Grey Cup: The Canadian Football League championship game, and the name of the trophy awarded to the winner

homesteaders: Prairie settlers

Métis: A group of people of mixed Aboriginal and European ancestry

mineral salts: Naturally occurring minerals that can increase the buoyancy of water

paleontologists: Scientists who study ancient fossils such as dinosaur remains

prairie: Natural grasslands, usually found in a dry, sunny climate

protected: Describes an animal species, plant species or geographic area that is being kept from harm

rampage: A violent and rushed attack

Rupert's Land: A territory named after Prince Rupert, a nephew of King Charles I. It was controlled by the Hudson's Bay Company from 1670 until 1870.

sinew: Tendons that connect muscle to bone

treason: An attempt to overthrow one's own ruler or government

treaty: A formal agreement between people or countries